THE SOLDIER THROUGH THE AGES

THE MEDIEVAL KNIGHT

Martin Windrow

Illustrated by
Richard Hoo

Franklin Watts
London   New York   Toronto   Sydney

© Franklin Watts Limited 1985

First published in Great Britain in 1985 by
Franklin Watts Ltd
12a Golden Square
London W1

First published in the USA by
Franklin Watts Inc.
387 Park Avenue South
New York
N.Y. 10016

First published in Australia by
Franklin Watts Australia
1 Campbell Street
Artarmon
NSW 2064

UK edition ISBN: 0 86313 180 8
US edition ISBN: 0-531-03834-8
Library of Congress Catalog Card
No: 84-52569

Designed by James Marks

Printed in Belgium

Contents

Lords of war

In what historians call the "high medieval" period, from about 1100 to 1500, Europe was often torn by wars – and wars were dominated by knights. This word is now used to mean a fighting man protected by metal armor, who rode into battle on a big war-horse.

In the early part of this period foot soldiers rarely played a serious part in pitched battles. Most were simple peasants,

▷ A 14th-century knight in full war harness displays the colors of his family. Noble families often had estates and alliances which crossed national frontiers. This made it harder for kings to ensure their loyalty. In the background an army leaves a village ravaged by war. Lords often provoked their enemies to fight by raiding their estates, killing, burning and looting without mercy. Life could be very cruel for the common people.

more or less badly armed, trained and organized. The heavy, armored rider, charging down on them like a human rhinoceros, often scattered them in panic. Serious fighting was usually left to the opposing knights.

In this period Europe was divided into many small nations. Although trade was growing, farmland, flocks and herds were the only real source of wealth. Kings did not have the money to pay permanently organized armies – certainly not armies of knights, whose armor and horses were expensive. So they parceled out land among their barons, the powerful, aristocratic families in their kingdoms. Taxes and farm revenues enriched the barons; and in return for their estates they provided knights for the king's wars.

In fact it took a strong king to rule these powerful, arrogant barons. Quarrelsome and violent, they often rebelled. Costly feuds among family alliances were common. Wars between countries were frequent too. Most were simply attempts by kings to take over neighboring territories.

Privilege and protection

Medieval Europe was peopled by the mass of poor peasants and a small land-holding nobility whose fields they worked. Under what we now call the feudal system, the king was supposed to own all land. He divided it among powerful lords who became his vassals. This meant that in return for land, they swore loyalty to the king and agreed to provide soldiers.

The lords, in turn, divided much of their land among less wealthy knights, in return for the same bargain. The knight might be rich, or the poor squire of a single tumble-down village. But whatever his wealth, he was part of the only class privileged to hold land and bear arms.

Barons and knights lived off the labor of their peasants and the taxes paid by towns-people. They administered the law and had great power over the peasants in their territories. In return, in accordance with the code of chivalry, they were supposed to protect the weak in time of war.

In fact they usually caused more misery than they prevented. Chivalry was shown to their own class, but seldom to the common folk. As knights were brought up to believe that fighting was the only proper occupation, they often provoked wars. They had little else to do than pursue "glory" in war, acquire more land and spend their wealth on lavish displays of splendor and luxury.

▽ Medieval nobles enjoy the sport of hawking while peasants clear their fields. Common people had to work their lords' land without pay for several days a week. They paid a share of the produce of their own small patches to their lord and to the church. More cash was raised by taxes on shopkeepers, on the use of mills and wine-presses, on people using the law courts, and on people's goods when they died. The raising of new kinds of tax caused much resentment.

Castles

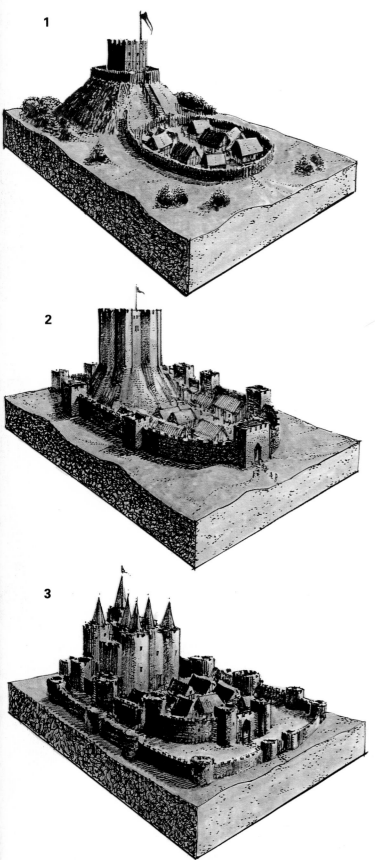

Kings and lords ruled their lands from castles. Serving as both palace and prison, a castle was also a military fortress to guard the borders. In the eleventh century castles were usually built of timber. By the next century the central tower, or keep, and the walls surrounding the yards and outbuildings were usually being rebuilt in massive stonework.

Early medieval armies used siege machines much like those of the ancient Greeks and Romans, including catapults, battering rams and siege towers. Stone castles did sometimes fall to outright assault, but treachery or starvation were often more effective than actual storming.

Because only the ruins of most castles remain today, we tend to think of them as cold, damp, dreary places to live. In fact they were often gaily painted inside and out, and well furnished. They had many fires, and windows were covered with shutters, sheets of transparent parchment or even glass. In time, even the soldiers' guardrooms were fitted with washbasins and toilets!

◁ **1** Timber castle of c.1075. The main tower is built on a mound, or motte; the outbuildings are in a walled yard, or bailey.
2 Rebuilt in stone, c.1200. The massive central keep is protected by "curtain" walls, with smaller towers spaced along them.
3 Vastly enlarged, c.1300, the castle was almost impregnable – until the invention of artillery.

▷ A page serves the lords and ladies at a castle banquet. At the age of seven, a knight's son was sent away to the castle of a relative or family friend. There he was taught the manners of a nobleman and the code of chivalry. In return he served as a page, fetching and carrying and waiting on tables. It was not a pampered childhood, no matter how wealthy the boy's background.

A school of hard knocks

At fourteen, if he showed promise, a boy who had served as a page was made a squire. This was the personal servant of a knight. His duties included cleaning and caring for his knight's armor, weapons and other possessions, and he accompanied the knight on campaign as a camp servant.

In return, the youngster was taught the skills of a fighting man. This was the only profession for a well-born boy. He became gradually accustomed to wearing heavy armor, and was taught how to handle sword and lance in battle. He also learned, painfully, that managing a powerful stallion in combat was nothing like jogging along on a fat pony!

At eighteen he could be knighted himself by his feudal lord, often in a church ceremony. After spending a night alone at prayer, he was presented with his sword and spurs. This marked his new status as a "gentle, worthy, faithful and devoted knight," sworn to defend churches, orphans, widows "and all the servants of God."

▷ In the courtyard of a castle young squires are trained by experienced soldiers. Fighting with sword, lance and poleaxe took strength and agility. Armor was hot and tiring to wear; by the time he was knighted a boy had to be able to endure it for hours of exercise. Plate and mail armor weighed between 50 and 70 lb (22–32 kg). But it is not true that a fallen knight was as helpless as a turned turtle! Unless he was stunned or wounded, a knight could move easily – he had to, if he was to fight effectively. Knights even used to show off by doing energetic tricks in full armor.

The permanent garrisons of castles included poorer knights, and low-born sergeants, who were paid and kept by their lord. The oath of loyalty also required tenant knights to serve as castle guards for several weeks each year.

Training with a quintain
The squire had to hit the target shield and then duck quickly, or the swinging weight would knock him off his horse.

Men of iron

Between the 1100s and the late 1400s there were enormous changes in the design of armor. Most of these developments were to do with combat efficiency rather than the changing styles of fashion. Nevertheless, there were rich knights who loved to display their wealth by wearing beautiful gilded and jeweled armor.

Twelfth-century knights wore ring mail all over their bodies, with big, bucket-shaped helmets. However, it was found that ring-mail did not give very good

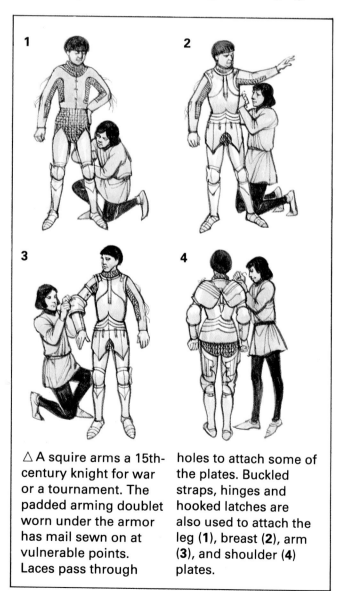

△ A squire arms a 15th-century knight for war or a tournament. The padded arming doublet worn under the armor has mail sewn on at vulnerable points. Laces pass through holes to attach some of the plates. Buckled straps, hinges and hooked latches are also used to attach the leg (**1**), breast (**2**), arm (**3**), and shoulder (**4**) plates.

protection and could be pierced by a sharp sword point. Knights of the 1200s began to add extra metal plates and thickly padded fabric over the top of the mail. At first these covered the knees, elbows and shoulders. During the 1300s more and more plates were added to cover other parts of the body. The smiths who made armor gradually learned how to shape and fit the plates to give better protection against different kinds of weapons.

By the 1400s the plates were no longer separate pieces strapped one by one to the limbs and body. They were starting to join up into complete suits. The different plates were attached to each other by straps, and by rivets which slid up and down carefully placed slots, so that one plate moved easily against the next as the knight flexed his limbs. The surfaces also featured ribs which caught the points of weapons and sent them skidding off harmlessly. Helmets were now smaller and lighter, with movable visors over the face. Ring mail was now used only in awkward areas, such as the groin and armpits, where plates could not be shaped to fit conveniently.

◁ **Far left** An Italian knight, Sir Galeotto Malaspina of Verona, *c.*1360. His mixed armor of mail, steel plates and hardened leather is typical of the experiments tried by armorers in the 14th century. A neck-guard of mail on padded cloth is joined to the bascinet helmet. Chains attached to the chest prevented him losing his weapons in battle.

◁ **Left** This knight of the 1480s wears a complete suit of steel plate battle armor. Many separate plates are cleverly fitted together, protecting the whole body but sliding over one another so smoothly that the knight could move easily. It was vital that such a suit was fitted exactly to the knight's measurements, for steel does not stretch!

War games

Medieval knights lived for fighting; and since, even in those violent times, wars were not continuous, they held many mock battles or tournaments in time of peace.

At an appointed day and place knights would gather to display their strength and skill against one another. Sometimes they fought massed combats in large groups; sometimes individuals would pair off, on foot or on horseback. In the thirteenth century so many men were being killed in these mock battles that it became a public scandal. One tournament at Cologne in 1240 cost 60 lives! The Pope decreed that the slaughter must stop, and it became customary to fight with special blunted weapons. Although plate armor protected contestants from most injuries other than flesh wounds and broken bones, accidental deaths were still common.

Knights fought under supervision, according to strict rules. Tournaments became dazzling social occasions, with crowds cheering on their favorite champions. Apart from the glory and the official prizes, the winners were usually awarded the losers' costly armor and horses. This was a lure which brought poor knights

flocking to try their skill in hopes of bettering their fortune.

The best-known type of combat was the tilt, in which two knights charged one another with lances. Very heavy, oddly shaped armor was worn for greater safety. Some even had sprung panels which flew off to signal an accurate hit!

◁ A group of 15th-century knights fight on foot in "the barriers," a common tournament bout.

△ By about 1150 knights began to paint family symbols on their shields to identify friend from foe. These developed into the complex system of heraldry. Shields, surcoats, and banners identified not only a family, but even individual members. The illustration above shows the personal standard, shield, helmet crest and family retainers' badge of Henry Stafford, Earl of Wiltshire, c.1460.

Raising an army

The raising of troops was supposed to be easy and cheap under the feudal system. The king summoned his barons to supply the number of men agreed under the terms of their oath. The baron assembled men from his own household troops and called in his tenant knights. Each knight was bound to report for a set number of days' service with a specified number of fully equipped men from his estates.

In fact this system broke down as early as the 1200s. Knights enjoyed fighting – but they preferred to pick their own time and their own quarrels! In practice the king had to offer cash pay to most of his followers. So armies of the fourteenth and fifteenth centuries were very mixed affairs indeed.

There were lords who obeyed the old feudal summons; but for serving more than the customary 40 days – seldom long enough to be of any use, especially in a foreign war – they expected to be offered money as well. Some would accept a large cash contract from the king, using the money to hire paid volunteers.

▷ Each English shire was bound by law to send certain numbers of men to war. During the Hundred Years' War with France, from 1338 to 1453, there was seldom any shortage of volunteers. Apart from the lure of adventure and loot, an archer could earn as much as a skilled craftsman – threepence a day in 1346, and sixpence by the late 1300s. This was impressive, in comparison with twelve pence a day for a mounted, partly armored cavalryman.

By law, only eldest sons inherited land, so there were usually many landless young knights happy to take pay for joining the army's heavy cavalry or for leading groups of paid troops.

The money paid to lords and kings for letting their vassals off personal service could also be used to hire professional mercenary soldiers. Such men were often foreigners, with better-than-average training and discipline.

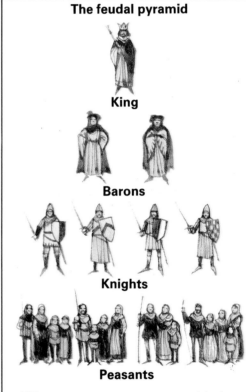

The feudal pyramid

King

Barons

Knights

Peasants

When most troops were provided by feudal service – raising men from "the next level down" – kings had few reliable troops of their own. In theory everybody owed the king personal loyalty; in fact kings ruled only by consent of the barons. Strong kings easily persuaded the nobles to support them; weak kings lost their thrones, and lives, in barons' rebellions.

The deadly mêlée

Once armies actually came face to face, most medieval battles were confused affairs. There was little thought for clever tactics: the fighting was more like a football practice than a game of chess! Armies were often roughly divided into three groups which commanders tried to send into action one after another. But knights were impatient of orders, and often ruined any overall plan by charging as soon as they saw the enemy.

To the knight, the whole point of warfare was to charge full-tilt into battle, jostling for a place in the front rank. Displaying his own strength and courage was more important than winning any particular battle for his lord and king.

The 1400s saw commanders making slow progress in forcing their knights to obey a disciplined plan. This became easier as more and more knights fought for cash wages.

◁In a 14th-century battle knights ride down foot soldiers in their eagerness to get within a sword's length of each other. Foot soldiers were very useful when they were given a chance. If properly trained and organized, they could be a deadly threat to the knight.

The knight killers

In the mid-1300s the knight began to face two challenges to his mastery of the battlefield: the use of trained foot soldiers with long-range weapons, and the appearance of the first guns. Most knights tried to ignore the problem; they thought the new methods very unsporting, if not downright immoral! But ignoring them did not make them go away.

Early medieval foot soldiers, recruited among farm laborers for only weeks at a time, often had no proper training. In battle they sometimes behaved like sheep, because they were not told what they were expected to do, or shown how to do it. They often missed the battle altogether, because the knights rushed ahead. Usually, they were frightened of the men on horses. Brought up to obey their proud masters, they often ran as soon as the opposing knights began to thunder toward them.

However, there were instances of battles in which the foot soldier played a more important role. The victory of Welsh archers at Falkirk in 1298, and that of Swiss poleaxe-men at Morgarten in 1339, persuaded some commanders to take infantry more seriously. If foot soldiers had weapons with a longer "reach" than a knight's lance, and if the men were taught to keep their nerve and stand together in a close-packed mass, then there was very little a knight could do to them. No horse, however excited, willingly charges a hedge of steel spearheads or a shower of arrows.

The tough Swiss mountaineers had very few knights; but they did have huge pikes, up to 18 ft (5.5 m) long. Packed together, they made a huge steel "hedgehog" no knight could break. They also learned how to keep their ranks tight even when running forward – and swept the enemy knights right off the battlefield.

The same success could be achieved by men shooting missile weapons at long range, provided they were protected by some sort of barricade so that the horsemen could not charge them down while they reloaded. English peasants were encouraged to practice with the longbow by the banning of all other Sunday sports.

Italians favored the crossbow. This short, strong bow mounted across a handle was pulled by a mechanical hook or lever. It was slower to reload than a longbow, but its heavy arrows could punch right through armor with terrible force.

The first crude hand-guns, which appeared in the 1360s, were too unwieldy and inaccurate to make much difference in battle. But they improved steadily, and by 1500 they had become a real threat.

◁ Crossbowmen carried large pavise shields, with props that left both hands free for the bow.

▽ Swiss halberdiers and pikemen hired themselves out as mercenaries all over Europe.

▽ Longbowmen, protected by sharp stakes from a sudden charge, could shoot six arrows a minute.

Like other missile weapons, early hand-guns were only effective if fired by many soldiers all at once.

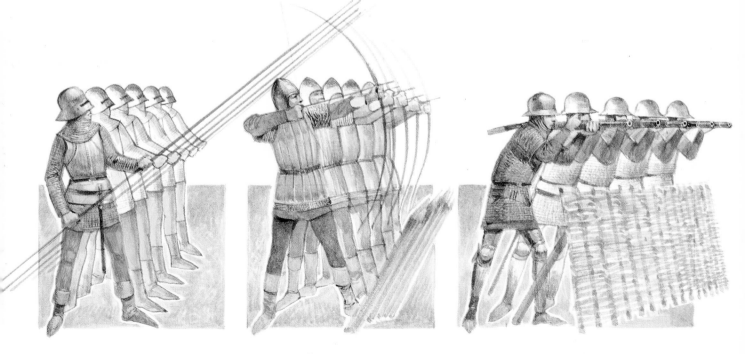

The arrow storm

In the Hundred Years' War English knights were greatly outnumbered by the French. Yet they still won great victories, like Crécy, Poitiers and Agincourt. Their "secret weapon" was the peasant armed with a longbow.

The bow itself was nothing new. But English leaders – such as Edward III, the Black Prince and Henry V – made it a war-winning tool by daring to arm peasants with a weapon which could defeat knights. It had to be used by many men together to be effective, so hired mercenaries were not sufficient. Thousands of English peasants had to be taught to use the bow if English armies were to be strong enough; and they had to be well paid and decently treated to persuade them to enlist when needed. Skilled archery took years of practice, and could not be simply enforced by brutality.

Battles were won by knights and archers fighting together according to an intelligent plan. Battlefields were carefully picked to make the most of the strengths of each (as in the plan in the diagram below). Credit for victory belonged as much to the archers as to the knights, and they learned to respect one another as comrades.

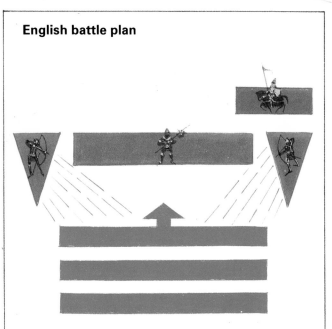

English battle plan

With flanks guarded by woods and marsh, dismounted English knights wait for French attack (blue). At each flank, wedges of archers can shoot ahead and inwards as the enemy get close. French knights are channeled into a narrow, packed crowd. Their greater numbers are no advantage: few can get into fighting range at any one time – while all are inside arrow range. Mounted English reserves await a chance to turn the enemy's defeat into a rout and to ward off any surprise attacks.

▷ At Crécy in 1346 about 12,000 French knights made repeated, brave, but doomed charges against some 3,000 English knights and 8,000 bowmen. Hedges, wagons, and holes to trip horses were used as a barrier to stop the French reaching the English line before they came under fire from a deadly arrow storm. The archers could put about 48,000 shafts into the air in just one minute. The slim bodkin arrowheads pierced mail and killed horses at over 110 yd (100 m). Closer up, they punched right through plate armor. About 1,500 French knights fell.

Ransom and ruin

Medieval soldiers on campaign often died of diseases like cholera and typhus – the great English King Henry V was one victim. The causes of disease and infection were not understood, and there were so few doctors that only the rich were treated. The chances of recovery from the horrible wounds caused by steel blades and spikes were not high. Broken bones could be set, fevers controlled, and cuts sewn up; but wounds were not properly cleaned, and many men died from later infections.

For common soldiers, good luck and a strong body were the only remedies. Badly hurt men died where they lay. Others might recover through the rough kindness of comrades, or the herbal medicines of a village healer.

▽ Taking this knight's right gauntlet – the token of surrender for ransom – has made these humble soldiers rich for life. Poor men dreamed of making their fortunes in this way, and were not usually cheated out of ransoms by their lords. The capture is listed by a herald, an official who recorded family coats-of-arms and also acted as an ambassador.

▷ A knight returns home to ruined estates.

Commoners taken prisoner might be killed right away, or turned loose after being deliberately mutilated as a warning to others. Things were very different for the knights, however.

Knights were usually taken alive and held for ransom whenever possible. The knight often lived more like a guest than a prisoner while awaiting ransom. All knights thought of other knights as social equals, to be treated chivalrously. But the wait could still be long and weary; and the cost might be so high that many knights eventually returned home to find lifelong debts awaiting them and their families.

France's King Jean and 2,500 of his knights were held for ransom by the English after Poitiers in 1356. The King's ransom was three million gold pieces; and all the ransoms together are said to have bankrupted France for twenty years.

The cost of ransoms, spread through money-lenders and town taxes, filtered down to the peasants in higher prices. At the same time, defeat left them even more helpless; many cruel bandits and paid-off soldiers roamed France, pillaging and murdering at will. Peasants bitterly resented the knights' failure, and some even attacked their lords when they finally returned.

The first paid companies

French defeats between 1340 and 1440 showed up the weaknesses of many medieval armies. But the French learned from their mistakes, and took steps to cut out the waste and confusion which had led to so many disasters. Other European armies were doing the same, and the first signs of permanent, regularly paid, disciplined, national troops began to appear. It was to be many years before Europe was to see the birth of the modern "standing army," but the first steps were at last being taken.

In 1439 Charles VII of France raised the first Royal Ordinance Companies. These were units of knights and infantry, paid for out of royal taxes levied on the regions where they were stationed. Each had a set number of men, and the types of armor and weapons were specified by the King. Well disciplined, they were answerable not to local lords, but only to the King, who chose and paid their leaders. These companies did much to help France win back all she had lost to the English since the 1340s.

Another impressive example of this new thinking was the army raised by the Dukes of Burgundy. By the late fifteenth century the Burgundian army was organized according to a set of regulations which were fussy enough to satisfy a government official. Complicated rules were drawn up to cover every possible subject – including how many days' leave a soldier could have, whose signatures he had to obtain on his ticket before he could go, and the scale of fines he had to pay if he was late back!

◁ The smallest unit in the new, paid companies was a lance. In the Burgundian army a lance was made up of one knight, two more lightly equipped riders, three mounted archers (who rode to war, but fought on foot), and an infantry pikeman, crossbowman and hand-gunner. Each hundred lances made up a company of 900 men, 600 of them mounted and 300 on foot.

The dawn of artillery

The first cannon appeared in the 1320s. At first they fired large arrows, with brass "feathers," at crowded enemy troops. Later in the fourteenth century stone and lead balls were used, and guns came to be fired mainly at castle walls during sieges. They were heavy and unwieldy, difficult to aim accurately and slow to load. They were only really useful when an army could settle down in one spot for weeks at a time in front of a large target like a castle.

A big gun, its ammunition and other equipment might need six wagons, 100 horses and 70 men just to travel across country at 10 miles (15 km) a day. Medieval dirt roads were so bad that gangs of workmen had to travel with the guns, mending the surface as they went.

As time passed, guns became lighter, more accurate and more reliable. Even so, gunpowder was still said to be "the invention of the Devil." Knights despised "cowards" who killed at a distance, with bullet or arrow, instead of risking "honorable" hand-to-hand combat. Perhaps they realized that if low-born men could defeat their social betters with these new weapons, the days of the knight were drawing to a close.

▷ Protected by entrenchments, a master gunner supervises artillery during a siege of c.1470. This highly paid expert is shouting at the crew of a bombard who have burst the gun by using too much powder. It will take weeks to move it to the workshop and repair it.

The burst gun shows why we use the words "gun barrel." The largest iron guns could not then be cast in one piece. They were made like barrels, with iron staves bound together by iron rings, and heated to melt the joints. Hidden weaknesses made many guns burst in action.

The smaller gun is a serpentine, a much more mobile type invented in c.1430.

Glossary

Arming doublet Padded cloth jacket, often with sections of ring-mail reinforcement, worn under a suit of armor.

Bailey The outer courtyard of a castle, containing stores, stables and other buildings.

Baron A medieval lord, holding large estates from his king.

Bascinet Fairly small helmet, shaped to send enemy blows glancing off its surface.

Bodkin arrowhead Slim, unbarbed arrowhead, usually triangular or square in section, for penetrating armor.

Bombard Heavy type of medieval cannon.

Chivalry Complicated code of behavior for knights, based on telling the truth, keeping one's word and protecting those weaker than oneself.

Coat-of-arms Set of heraldic devices which identified a medieval aristocrat's family. It was displayed in various ways on shields, surcoats and horse-hangings.

Crest Heraldic family symbol, modeled in light wood or leather, and worn on the helmet – though probably more often in tournaments than in actual battles.

Crossbow Short, powerful bow fixed across a shoulder-stock. The string was pulled back by a hook on the belt, or by a mechanical lever or crank.

Curtain wall The outer wall of a medieval castle.

Feudal system The way most European nations were organized in the early medieval period. Lords held land granted to them by their king in return for oaths of loyalty and providing agreed numbers of soldiers.

Garrison The group of soldiers who guarded a castle or town.

Gauntlet Armored glove worn by a knight.

Heraldry System of family identification symbols used by medieval aristocrats.

Keep The main tower or central redoubt of a medieval castle.

Lance Long spear used by a knight on horseback; it was braced rigidly under the right arm when they charged the enemy. Lance is also the name for the smallest unit of a 15th-century standing army, usually made up of one or more horsemen and a few foot soldiers.

Longbow Simple wooden bow, about the height of a man, favored by English and Welsh archers. Pulling a yew-wood war bow was equivalent to lifting a weight of between 80 and 120 lb (40–60 kg).

Mail (ring mail) Flexible type of armor made of many small iron rings linked into continuous sheets. It gave good protection against cuts with the edge of a blade, but a pointed weapon could burst through it.

Mercenary A man who fights as a profession, for any commander or country who will pay him.

Missile weapon Any weapon – such as a bow or gun – which throws something through the air at the enemy.

Motte The mound of earth on which a castle keep was built.

Pavise Large shield, with a prop which enabled it to be set up on the ground without being held.

Pike Large spear used by foot soldiers, for thrusting rather than for throwing.

Plate armor Armor made up of shaped sheets of metal.

Quintain Medieval training machine. Hitting the target made a weight swing around, which the soldier had to duck.

Ransom Sum of money demanded for the release of a prisoner.

Retainer Soldier permanently paid, or retained to be part of a baron's personal family army.

Sergeant Soldier of humble birth who fought on horseback alongside knights, often in rather cheaper and simpler armor.

Serpentine Light type of 15th-century cannon, fixed on its own wheeled carriage.

Squire Personal body-servant and apprentice to a knight.

Standard Long, narrow flag bearing the personal – rather than the family – devices of a medieval lord.

Standing army An army which is paid to serve continuously, rather than being called up only in wartime.

Surcoat Cloth jerkin worn over armor, sometimes with heraldic decoration.

Tilt The tournament event in which two knights on horseback charged one another with lances.

Tournament Mock battle between groups or individuals, very popular among medieval knights.

Vassal Under the feudal system, a man who held land as a tenant from a more powerful man, in return for oaths of loyalty and military service.

Visor Hinged face-plate on the front of a medieval helmet, pierced with slits and holes for vision and breathing.

Only major events in England and France are shown; minor wars and rebellions were continual.

1277–82 Edward I defeats the Welsh.

1296 Edward I defeats Scots at Dunbar.

1298 Sir William Wallace's Scots defeated by Edward's archers at Falkirk.

1314 Robert Bruce routs English at Bannockburn. Scottish independence recognized in 1328.

1338 Edward III's claim to throne of France causes Hundred Years' War.

1346 Edward III's son the Black Prince wins victory over French at Crécy.

1356 During one of several great raids across France, Black Prince defeats and captures French King Jean II at Poitiers. France suffers civil war and peasant revolts.

1381 Peasants' Revolt in England, during reign of weak King Richard II, is crushed.

1402–1403 Campaigns in Scotland and Wales by usurping King Henry IV and his son, later Henry V.

1415 Henry V wins great victory over French at Agincourt.

1429 Joan of Arc leads French to break English siege of Orléans. Charles VII crowned king of France. Although Joan is burned in 1431, French energy and confidence revive.

1448–53 Series of victories wins back for France almost all the previous English gains. End of Hundred Years' War.

1455–85 Long civil wars – Wars of the Roses – devastate England. Final victory of Henry VII founds Tudor dynasty. Barons stripped of much of their power. Medieval period ends.

Index

PRINTED IN BELGIUM BY

proost
INTERNATIONAL BOOK PRODUCTION